The Poetry Of Robert Nichols
Volume 2 – A Faun's Holiday

'O Fantaisie, emporte-moi sur tes ailes pour désennuyer
ma tristesse!' FLAUBERT.

Robert Malise Bowyer Nichols was born in September 1893.

Robert was educated at Winchester College and then Trinity College, Oxford. In September 1914
with the shadow of the Great War covering Europe he enlisted, despite poor health, with the Field
Artillery. He trained for a year and reached the front line just before the beginning of the Battle of
Loos in September 1915. He was also to serve at the Battle of the Somme as an artillery officer in
1916, after suffering from shell shock he was invalided back to England.

Taking up service with The British Ministry of Labour and the Ministry of Information he began to
write more avidly. As one of the War's surviving poets he was able to also give his work a depth and
reflection that many of his other fallen contemporaries were not able too. He also began to give
readings of his poems as well as tours in America.

Robert also wrote four plays and two novels as well as several further volumes of poetry. Now
rightly regarded as one of the pre-eminent War Poets his poetry is richly rewarding, filled with vivid
descriptions and emotions of the human suffering during war.

It's end brought him together with Nancy Cunard who was the inspiration for his next book Aurelia
(1920). He was in Tokyo from 1921 to 1924 teaching English Literature and from 1924 to 1926
Hollywood beckoned.

In 1928 his play, Wings Over Europe, foretelling the splitting of the atom was a success in New York.
In 1933-4 he was in Austria and Germany, his long weekly letters to Henry Head, the neurologist
under whose care he had been for shell-shock, give a graphic eye-witness account of the rise of
Hitler.

By the end of the 1930's he was living in the South of France, his emotional and financial affairs in
turmoil. With occupation of France by German and Vichy forces he was on the last ship to carry
British refugees from the Cote d'Azur.

Robert Nichols died on December 17th 1944. He is buried at St Mary's, in Lawford, Essex.

Index Of Contents

Poet's Notes.
Roughly planned in Spring, 1914, at Oxford. "Midday in Arcadia" composed July, 1914; "Catch for
Spring" adapted from version of 1912 during the same month: both at Grayshott. Taken up again in

February, 1916, continued at the Hut, Bray, and, after being frequently interrupted, finished on February 18, 1917, at Ilsington.

The author intends the "hulli" and the "lulli" of the Faun's call in 'Faun's Rally' to be pronounced as if they rhymed with such a word as "fully."

A FAUN'S HOLIDAY

I

Hark! a sound. Is it I sleep?
Wake I? or do my senses keep
Commune yet with thoughtful night
And dream they feel, not see, the light
That, with a chord as if a lyre
Were upward swept by tongues of fire,
Spreads in all-seeing majesty
Over crag, dale, curved shore, and sea?

If this be sleep, I do not sleep.
I hear the little woodnote weep
Of a shy, darkling bird which cries
In a sweet-fluted, sharp surprise
At glimpse of me, the faun-beast, sleeping
Nigh under her. My crook'd leg, sweeping
Some dream away, perhaps, awoke her,
For dew shook from a bough doth soak her.

And all elsewhere how still it is!
The mist beyond the precipice
Smokes gently up. The bushes hang
Over the gulph 'cross which I sprang
Last midnight, though the unicorn,
Who with clanged hooves and lowered horn
Raging pursued, now hidden lies
Amid the cragside dewberries
And sweats his frosty flanks in sleep,
Dreaming he views again my leap
Thrice hazardous.
The silver chasm
Sighs, and many a blithe phantasm
Turns in the sunlight's quivering ray.
I couch in peace. Thoughts fond and gay
Feed on my sense of maiden hours
And earth refreshed by suns and showers
Of nightly dew and heavy quiet.
Though last night rang with dinning riot:
Dionysos in headlong mood
Ranged through the labyrinthine wood;
Fleet maids sped, yelping, on with him,
Brandishing a torn heifer's limb,

Of the Faun's
Awakening.

Dissonant cymbals, or black bowl
Of wine and blood; a wolfish howl
Fled ululant with them....
Now there is
Depth, the white mist, the great sun, peace.

Too numb such sunshine! Let me hence
Out of the solemn imminence
Of yon chill spire whose shadow creeps
Toward me from the stagnant deeps
Of the ravine. For now I will
Descend and take again my fill
Of fancy wild and musing joy,
Such as each dawn brings to alloy
The long affliction of a spirit
Who a complete world did inherit,
And feels it crumbling.
I will down
Whither twin bluffs of sheer stone frown
Over sunk seas of billowing pine
Terrace on terrace, line on line,
Below whose heads the broad downs slope
Away, away till senses grope
At something rather felt than seen:
The sea, not wave-tops, but a sheen
Under the dazed and distant sky....
Curled on a cliff-top let me lie.
(For yonder, hap, a breeze is blowing,
And the sun's first gleam is showing
Under far wreckage: since our height
Inherits day while yet their light
Quakes gold under the low clouds' rift.)
Down, then! Miraculously swift
These limbs the gods have given me!...
Couched mid the gorse, anon I see,
Opposing this my bluff, the face
Of the sheer rock, and 'long it trace
A sill scarce ample for a goat,
Yet midway in the ledge-path note
A cave's mouth, which thick creepers hide
Fallen in a silvery tide
From a slant crevice overhead.
And, lo! the creeper stirs, is shed
And all falls quiet.
Till at last
Issues a voice deep, young and vast:

Of the Faun's
Descent from
the Mountain.

II

Centaur. Up! the ag'd centaurs lie yet sleeping,
While crouch I palled of this cavern lair

THE CENTAUR'S

And watch the stretched sea-eagle sweeping
Down the grey-blue drizzling air.
The sea-nymphs, too, will now be waking,
If sickle-eyed they have not played
Across the moonlight sets me aching,
Longing and slinking, half afraid,
Down the feathery, tawny sand
On sighing tread
Deep into banks of glistering shell,
To halt in dread
Lest my hoof-scrunch break the spell
Of the syren-chants that swell
From the dim shoals toward the land.

But this morn the breeze is blowing
Freshly: I hear lightly flowing
From the bending giant beam
Bars the forehead of our door
The golden raindrops in a stream
Pattering on the steamy floor.

Faun. It is the Centaur's voice I hear!
Young and lusty, deep and clear:
And the Panisks at his voice
In their fastnesses rejoice,
Emerging from the creviced crag
Or cave beneath the mountain's jag,
Merry, shaggy, light of hoof,
To run along the narrow roof,
And upon the shelvèd height
Dance before the swimming light.

Centaur. And I see upon the ledge,
Astir over the hanging edge,
A russet briar cold with dew
And beyond, forlornly pent
In a grey cloud's gliding rent,
A pure pool of the brightest blue:
So near it seems I've but to cast
A flint out on the forward vast
To mark it flashing blithely through!

And now at last!
At last
The great Sun,
The Sudden One,
Stamps upon the cloudy floor;
The heavens are split, and through the floor
Heaven's golden treasures tumbling pour....
And the Sun himself, divine,
Doth descend

MORNING SONG.

THE CENTAUR'S
MORNING SONG
(continued)

In such a bursting blaze of shine
That his glorious hair is shook
Over the wide world's craggiest end!
And, even I, I dare not look.

I will shout! I will ramp!
Just three bounds: then out and stamp
Where the air like water is
Eddying up over the precipice;
Wind with an edge to it, sea-damp,
Blowing from the canyon's race
Where the dripping sea-wind heaves
Through a tunnel of the rocks
Sea-water up in thunderous sheaves
Against the precipitous water-rapids,
To whip from off th' high-hurtled shocks
Bursts of mist which soak the leaves
Of each scented bush that cleaves
To the cliffs. Till Fauns and Lapiths
Dance in the sun-bewildered brakes,
Till even flushed Silenus wakes,
And with a short deep-throated troll
To the wind and to the wine,
Both delirious, both divine!
Starts, as he drains the tilted bowl,
At din, to rolling uproar grown,
Of rocks dislodged and bounding down,
With splinter of pines and flint-shocked flashes,
From the ridge whereon we dance
In a loud exuberance
Of rattling hoofs whose echoes drown
The squealing joy or reedy pining
Of Pan's pipe, where Pan reclining
Plays in the clouded mountain's crown!

III

Faun. It is the Centaur's voice I hear.
The creeper tresses toss with fear,   The Faun hails
Then part before a pow'rful hand.   the Centaur.
See, see, O see the Centaur stand
With ruggëd head erect and proud,
Whose rounded mouth yet chants aloud
The Joy of Mind fulfilled in Force:
Glory of Man, glory of Horse.

Hail thou, the sov'reign of the hill!
Hail thou, upon whose locks distil
Fresh dews when mid majestic night
Thou pacest, hid, along the height.
Thine are the solitudes of snow

Between bare peaks, thy hooves also
Are heard within the dusk defile
Where Titans of a sunless while
Fashioned huge sphinxes in whose eyes
The Kite now skulks or, girding, cries.
Thine, too, the sole and sinking pine
Burned by the sunset, ay, and thine
The ledges whence a sudden sift
Of snow sighs downward, thine the swift
Uproar of avalanche and all
The mountain echoes. To thee call,
When the snow melts and there are seen
Crocuses blazing mid the green
Of the dewed grass, the Sylvan folk:
The Dryads from the leafless oak
Or budded elder, that at length
Thou mayst release them by the strength
Of thy tough fingers; 'tis on thee
The nymphs cry should the runnels be
Exhausted of the midsummer sun,
Sith, stamping, thou canst make to run
The hoarded waters of the wold.
And among men thou art of old
Thought's emblem: for to thee belong
All gifts of deep, wise, epic song.
Hail, then, whom Earth and mankind hails.
And Ocean, whose high-spouting whales
And dripping serpents, that arise
Swinging their gold crests to the skies
To drink in all thy bold descant
Hail, though they cannot view thee chant,
As I who now behold in sooth
Thy lighted eyes and singing mouth.

O grape-hung locks! glorious face,
Capacious frame, sinewy grace
Of arm that lifts a skully lyre
Whose dithyramb whirls ever higher!
Deep breast-bone, belly, curvèd thews
Such as the tussling oak doth use
Upon the crumbled scarp to grip
Striking from trunk down through the hip
Into the stallion's massive shoulders
Glossy as moonlit ice-bound boulders!
Stiff, stalwart forelegs, heavy hoof
Yet fleeter far on heights aloof
Than ev'n such doubled hares as race
Blue 'thwart dim fells, or, speck in space,
Osprey, gale-swept across the tides!
Thy man's trunk glisters; on thy sides
A soft and silver shagginess,

Of the Centaur's
Beauty.

Inviting slim hands to caress,
Hangs dewy

Centaur. Faun, Faun, art thou near?

Faun. Behold me stand, proud Centaur, here
Upon the bluff where 'neath me lies
The sunned pool of the precipice.

Centaur. Faun, in my veins the blood 'gins race,
The new sun sweats upon my face,   Of the
Dazzles my pupils, golden swims   Centaur's
Over my flushed and fervid limbs.   Ardour.
I feel in me my spirit rise
Griffon-like flogging up tall skies.
Now is the Morning of the World,
And through my heart a flood is hurled
Of onerous joyance, of desire
To clutch the sun and spill its fire
Down heaven's blue bulwarks! to snatch life
And drain its lusty full in strife
Of all my body with the bent
Wrestle of every element:
Close with the whirlwind, front the tide
And turn its moony press aside.

But in the world I cannot find
A match in strength, a foe in mind....
At dawn, at eve the waters burn;
All night the constellations turn
Round the dark pole, and none knows why....
None seeks to know save only I
And thou, O Faun. We are alone....
Yet sometimes, when the wind is gone
And all below shines sunned and still,
I feel depart from me the will
Merely to know, to know and wait:
I would do more: I would create.
Though what I know not; but I would
Spend this my mind and hardihood.
Yet find no means save physic force:
Sing as a man, stride as a horse.
Then stride I? Swift I overcome
The fleetest. Sing I? All are dumb.
Natheless my heart demands in grief
Ardour, endurance and relief;
Asks, but receives not.

Faun. Shall not I
Echo thy pain, whom Fates deny
Answer to thought, as they to thee

The lust-of-action's fill? But we
Accept too much, O Sire. 'Twere best,
Though idly, to fulfil our zest.

Four leagues this canyon runs between
Us twain or ever there is seen
The arch of rock whose massy grace
Bridges yon gap of golden space.
Deignest thou, then, to race with me
From such tall eyries to the sea,
If even now I upward leap?

Centaur. Leap then! I catch thee e'er the steep
Subsides in woodland or in down.

Of the
Challenge.

IV

Away! My rapping footfalls drown
All but the sobbing of the wind
Within my ears and loud behind
The thunder of the Centaur's hooves
Where, like a hailstorm, down he moves.
Past me the spun pines rock and hiss,
Behind my feet stones pelted whizz,
Hills rise before me, backward flow,
The bare downs, bright'ning, mount below....
On. On. Down. Down. But, ah, no more!
My breath comes keener than the frore
Indraught of age-long mountain frost;
My head turns dizzy, feet are lost.
Yet scamper feet! A rock, a mound:
Rap! Rap! I soar it at a bound.
On. On. Down. Down. A sudden brook,
And now, in mid-air, lo! there look
Laughingly up at me the eyes
Of Hyads, and their fading cries
Ring in my ears. Can they have seen
The Centaur hurtle by between
Them and the clouds? The downs up-fly.
Now earth's bowl rocks and reels the sky
And through my chilly flaming tears
The molten sun swoops, bursts, and veers....

And of the
Manner of
the Running.

Still rap my hoofs, though but the sound
Tells me they yet rocket the ground.
The uproar loudens more behind.
My crook'd legs cross, my eyes go blind.
I claw the sky: for, O! I can
Scarce lurch. I feel the sudden fan
Of the great Centaur's galey breath
Upon my nape, and like chill death

His hand descends. But, ah! he laughs
Even as Bacchus when he quaffs
In jest or taunt a double bowl.
I, choking, reel, and, tripping, roll   The Faun
Wildly aside. See! as I fall   falls.
A rampant shape majestical
Storms vehement by, and, storming, swings
Hand across rushing lyre, which rings
To strains, like rolling breakers tossed
High o'er an adamantine coast,
In praise of elemental Mirth,
Strength, Beauty and the Golden Earth!

V

Beyond the rocks, below the trees,   Of Downs
The great downs lie; nought but the breeze   beloved
Is heard upon them. All day long   by Pan.
The shadows of the great clouds throng
Across their sides: a noiseless rout.
Sometimes a peewit, blown about
By airy surge, cries a lone cry
Ere hurtled down the clarid sky;
Sometimes is heard a shepherd's voice
Shouting, and after it the noise
Of many-pattering crowded sheep
Herded within the gay dog's keep,
Who also, barking, shouts. Save these
Nought breaks the breezy silences
Of the green sun-swept, cloud-swept spaces....

Such downs Pan loves, and ofttime places
His lonely altars on them.
I
One of such now behold. A high
Mound bears it, and its nakedness
Of festal fruit and fragrant dress
Hints 'tis new-built.
Up, then, and sound
A rally to the sacred ground:

Faun. Come ye, merry shepherds all,
Hulli-lulli-li-lo!   FAUN'S RALLY.
Listen to my piping call:
Hulli-li-lo!
Hasten to Pan's festival;
Leave your sheep.
Cannot Pan a shrewd watch keep
O'er his own?
Safe are they as pent in stall;
Safe are they, for Pan has thrown

Fear about them like a wall.

Wherefore, shepherds, hither run.

I have set my pipes to lip;
Now they cry despondingly
As mid shaken locks I dip.
Now shrill, as hark! I lift them high
To swirl the tune about the sky!
Up and down and round the sky
Till want I further force to blow....
Wherefore, shepherds, hither run,
Dance behind me as I skip;
Strike the tóssed támbours in únison,
Dance, dance and make to dance the sun
To your Hulli-li-lo!

Shepherds. Faun, I come. I hear. We hear

Faun. This my Hulli-li-lo:
Now afar and now anear.

Shepherds. Never sped the midnight deer
Half so fast
'Fore Diana's star-ringed spear
As now haste we to appear
At thy Hulli-li-lo!

Faun. Joy, O shepherds, at the sound:
Hulli-lulli-li-lo!
Pan's new altar I have found:
Hulli-li-lo!
Cowslips prank its holy mound,
With ivy have I wreathed it round
But not yet
Is the altar's dress complete
Till with flowers its horns are bound.

Shepherds. Faun, we hear, and from the brook
Flags are pulled; and now we hook
Honeysuckle high, low
Down to us with shepherd's crook;
Breathing floss,
Clematis twines, rushy stook,
Apple blossom, down is shook
At thy Hulli-li-lo!

Faun. Wreathe the pedestal anew;
Hulli-lulli-li-lo!
Scatter violets scattering dew;
Hulli-li-lo!

Honey that the brown bees brew
Pour, and rosy blossoms strew;
Spill such wine
As in dim-bloomed clusters grew
On your father's father's vine.
Dance you now.
I my pipe cease, thus, to blow:
Dance you on.
Dance about the sacred mound,
Dance when every sound is gone....
Now the timbrels softly, sprightly
Beat, and foot it gaily, lightly;
Tiptoe o'er the secret ground,
Dance the round.

Next, to the sole, trilling flute
And your own subduèd laughter
Flutter all in throngs and mazes,
Chase in streams of ardent faces,
With bright eyes and oped mouth mute.
Now alone,
One by one,
Dance and dream, and dreaming float
Till the multitude drifts after,
And I wake a quicker note:
Clap your hands aloft and cry;
Surge in line tumultuously;
Cry, and with a whirl of voices
Fright the pigeons whickering by!
Praise the God of field and fold!
Shout until the hills have told,
By their sudden echoes flying,
Flying, crying, falling, dying,
That upon his name we call,
Who beside the river lying
Hears us keep his festival.

VI
Wearied of solitary hills,   The Faun enters
On which the wannish sunlight spills,   the Valley.
And which the glooms of high clouds cross,
Clouds wandering ever at a loss
About th' immeasurable sky,
I will descend. And by-and-by
Glimpse beneath the shouldered down
A hamlet reeking golden-brown;
Creep through a willow copse to view
Under an orchard avenue,
A lithe girl in a sun-splashed smock
Calling her perchèd pigeon flock,

And as they coo and flutter over
Laughing and carolling of her lover.

Girl. 'Little pigeon, grave and fleet'
All the golden grain you'd eat,
Greedy! let the little bird
Pick some. Sweet, your cooing's heard;
You shall have this. There! Be bolder:
Light you now upon my shoulder....
Cooroo? Cooroo in my ear?
Darling, yes, I hear, I hear:
From this hand, then, you shall pluck it.
Foolish love! your wings have struck it,
Spilt the grain the grass among.
Flutter! Flutter! where's my song?
'Little pigeon, grave and fleet'
Too late now your wings you beat
By my face: look in the ground;
There, they say, all gold is found.

Little pigeon, grave and fleet,   THE PIGEON SONG.
Eye-of-fire, sweet Snowy-wings,
Think you that you can discover
On what great green down my lover
Lies by his sunny sheep and sings?

If you can, O go and greet
Him from me; say: She is waiting....
Not for him, O no! but, sweet,
Say June's nigh and doves, remating,
Fill the dancing noontide heat
With melodious debating.

Say the swift swoops from the beam;
Soon the cuckoo must cease calling;
Kingcups flare beside the stream,
That not glides now but runs brawling;
That wet roses are asteam
In the sun and will be falling.

Say the chestnut sheds his bloom;
Honey from straw hivings oozes;
There's a nightjar in the coombe;
Venus nightly burns, and chooses
Most to blaze above my room;
That the laggard 'tis that loses.

Say the nights are warm and free,
And the great stars swarm above him;
But soon starless night must be.
Yet if all these do not move him,

Tell, O tell but not too plainly!
That I long for him and love him.

Little pigeon, grave and fleet,
Fly you swiftly, tell him this;
And I'll give you grain so golden
Midas' self has ne'er beholden
Aught so gold, and yes! a kiss.

Smiling at her eager voice,
I will grant the girl her choice,
Whispering to the pigeon: "Lo!
Yon's the way for you to go:
Over the willows, past the copse,
To where a sylph-like lime-tree tops
A lonely knoll; then on and on
Toward where yesternight there shone
A silver comet, scarce descried,
Against the fainting eventide."

VII

Away then! crashing through the wood,   Of the Faun's
Prancing in a whimsey mood,   Whimseys.
To yowl as a she-wolf does at dark
Until th' infuriate watch-dogs bark;
Or bid hushed tales of ghosts go round,
Of warnings heard, but nothing found,
By whistling at the village boor;
Or poke my rogue face round a door
And scare a huffy wife to fits,
Who swears, "'Tis Pan himself!" or, "It's
That grizzled sailor-man who slew
His mate 'twixt Bogs and Dead Man's Yew!"
Next through the dairy steal to slake
My thirst with cream, with honeycake
Cram my sweet maw; slip in the churn
A farm cat, that the tub may turn
And fright maid Molly. I will seek
Strawberries and stain chin, mouth and cheek
With nuzzling in their scarlet bowl;
Then in the goodman's bed I'll roll
Because he loves me not; I'll sing
Until the crowded rafters ring
The while about my ears I hang
Bobbed cherries.... Lastly I will clang
Among the clattering pots and pans,
Shout, cry "Oh help!" snatch up a man's
Cloak, and slip out.
Whoop! Whoop! They run: The Pursuit.
The hare once spied, the hunt's begun!

Goodman and goodman's wife, pert Polly,
Clown Colin, Wiggen and maid Molly,
Pant, crying, "Thief!" The while behind
Shrunk Dorcas hops, and fills the wind
With apish merriment, shrill malice,
And cries of "Well run, Poll! Run, Alice!
Run, child! The master's cloak and all!
How sad the goodman's ta'en a fall!
Mistress down, too, he! he! what pity!
Run, Alice child, my bird, my pretty;
Show 'em how nimble thou canst be,
Ay, but the girl runs prettily.
Run, Hobbinol, thou gawky man!
Thou mayest kiss if catch thou can!
Odd's me! and what's it all about?
A thief? That mischief Faun!"
A shout
Startles the pigeons from the croft:
"We've circled him!" "He's in the loft."
But as they, silent, crowd unto 't
I jump. For am not I a goat?
From out the hayloft's height I leap
O'er their craned heads into the deep
Grass of the orchard. Thence I run
Across lush meadows. One by one
They fall behind....
A scarecrow I
Now seek, and 'bout it carefully
Enwrap the newly pilfered cloak....
Scarecrows are such poor crazy folk....

VIII

So to a thorny thicket dense	The Faun
With rosy-coloured may-bloom, whence	hides.
I can hear a torrent rumble,	
And, peering forth, behold it tumble	
Cumbrously into a pool whose white	
Tumult sears the giddied sight.	
There, half dozed, silent, smile to hear	
A babble of voices drawing near,	
Spy many a boy and laughing lass	
Racing hands-linked across the grass.	

Boys and Girls. Now has the blue-eyed Spring	
Sped dancing through the plain.	A CATCH
Girls weave a daisy chain;	FOR SPRING.
Boys race beside the sedge;	
Dust fills the blinding lane;	
May lies upon the hedge:	
All creatures love the spring!	

The clouds laugh on, and would
Dance with us if they could;
The larks ascend and shrill;
A woodpecker fills the wood;
Jays laugh crossing the hill:
All creatures love the spring!

The lithe cloud-shadows chase
Over the whole earth's face,
And where winds ruffling veer
O'er wooded streams' dark ways
Mad fish upscudding steer:
All creatures love the spring!

Into the dairy cool
Run, girls, to drink thick cream!
Race, boys, to where the stream
Winds through a rumbling pool,
And your bright bodies fling
Into the foaming cool!
For we'll enjoy our spring!

IX

Seaward my forest way I'll take,
And at a pool's lit quietude slake
My thirst, and feel a dull flame creep
Like the first flux of tidal sleep
Through all my limbs. Yet, when I sink
Sleepward, start wide-eyed up to drink
The sunned wood's wet deliciousness,
Touch flowers, and feel the sun's caress
About my locks, and wander on,
Or pause to smile up at the sun,
Guarding my eyes with glowing hand,
Or, leaned against a beech-trunk, stand
Watching between the branches' rift,
As they gently wave and lift
To the bland breeze softly blowing,
The noiseless clouds serenely going
Slowly to the hid, low sea
I can hear breathing slumberously.
Till from the woodland I emerge,
Greeted by a louder surge,
And from the bushy cliff-top spy
How the hollow bay doth lie
One quiver and murmur under the sun,
And how the lightsome wind-puffs run
Chasing each other crookedly,
Over the idly heaving sea.

Of the Faun's
Journey to the Sea.

Next I will turn my eyes, perhaps,   Of the
To where the languid waters lapse   Sea-Horses.
Glittering over a sunburned rock
Round which the shrieking white gulls flock....
Thus browsing in my solitude,
I may remember I've a feud
With the Sea-Horses, once who drave
Me from the sea-light of their cave.
Enough! and, crashing down, I come
To find them drowsing in their home....
So creep I with a crooked stick
To where a blinding pool is quick
With green electric water-snakes.
Sprawling across a rock which bakes
I stir the molten till they boil
And up my hawthorn kick and coil;
Then scamper, rocketing, to the cave,
Hurl the stick in. Hark! how they rave,
And plunge up clattering, kicking, neighing,
Till Triton on his horn 'gins braying,
And each hasteneth to belabour
With hooves or tear with teeth his neighbour,
And from the cavern's blueness rush
Into the simmering beach's hush,
To stand, with heaving flanks, agaze
At the hot stones and still sea's blaze:
Then stampede, scattering high and wide
A hail of stones and glittering tide.

X
I will walk the sunny wood,   Of the Faun
Deep and tranquil as my mood,   in his
And watch how the honeyed sunlight is   Meditation.
Hung in the great boughs of the trees,
And the pattern the branchwork weaves
Under the panoply of leaves,
And how high up two butterflies
Pass, vaulting, out into the skies.
Or, entering a silent glade,
Draw a sharp breath and stand dismayed
At beauty which doth straight present
Such a spasm of ravishment
Sight is confused, and doth confess
Her wreck in voiceless tenderness:
Seeing the flower-decked cherry-trees
Unruffled ever by any breeze,
Unburned by bright dawn's fiery chill
Standing celestially still....

Or lay me down 'neath chestnut boughs,
And drowse and dream and dream and drowse,
Drunk with the greenness overhead,
Until a blossom of sharp red,
Shook from her high and scalding place,
Splash with chill scent my upturned face.

XI

But, lo! amid the woodland green   Of the
What mantles of strange blue are seen?   Philosopher.
What sage is he who slowly leads
Disciples on and little heeds
The holiness of sylvan haunt,
Where even the silver bird dare chant
But seldom? where the sunlight lies
Here scalding gold, and yonder dies
Into a humid, still, green gloom?
Hath not he in the forum room
To vent himself, that now with rude
Rabble he scareth Solitude
From her ultimate hiding-place?
Now steps he forward a slow pace,
And 'gins his discourse. Hear him prate,
O woods, to silence consecrate;
Hear him, O flowers, whose golden eyes
Speak more than all Man's orat'ries!

Philosopher. Meanwhile, though nations in distress
Cower at a comet's loveliness   And his
Shaken across the midnight sky;   Oration.
Though the wind roars, and Victory,
A virgin fierce, on vans of gold
Stoops through the cloud's white smother rolled
Over the armies' shock and flow
Across the broad green hills below,
Yet hovers and will not circle down
To cast t'ward one the leafy crown;
Though men drive galleys' golden beaks
To isles beyond the sunset peaks,
And cities on the sea behold
Whose walls are glass, whose gates are gold,
Whose turrets, risen in an hour,
Dazzle between the sun and shower,
Whose sole inhabitants are kings
Six cubits high with gryphon's wings
And beard and mien more glorious
Than Midas or Assaracus;
Though priests in many a hill-top fane
Lift anguished hands and lift in vain
Toward the sun's shaft dancing through

The bright roof's square of wind-swept blue;
Though 'cross the stars nightly arise
The silver fumes of sacrifice;
Though a new Helen bring new scars,
Pyres piled upon wrecked golden cars,
Stacked spears, rolled smoke, and spirits sped
Like a streaked flame toward the dead:
Though all these be, yet grows not old
Delight of sunned and windy wold,
Of soaking downs aglare, asteam,
Of still tarns where the yellow gleam
Of a far sunrise slowly breaks,
Or sunset strews with golden flakes
The deeps which soon the stars will throng.

For earth yet keeps her undersong
Of comfort and of ultimate peace,
That whoso seeks shall never cease
To hear at dawn or noon or night.
Joys hath she, too, joys thin and bright,
Too thin, too bright, for those to hear
Who listen with an eager ear,
Or course about and seek to spy,
Within an hour, eternity.
First must the spirit cast aside
This world's and next his own poor pride
And learn the universe to scan
More as a flower less as a man.
Then shall he hear the lonely dead
Sing and the stars sing overhead,
And every spray upon the heath
And larks above and ants beneath;
The stream shall take him in her arms;
Blue skies shall rest him in their calms;
The wind shall be a lovely friend,
And every leaf and bough shall bend
Over him with a lover's grace.
The hills shall bare a perfect face
Full of a high solemnity;
The heavenly clouds shall weep, and be
Content as overhead they swim
To be high brothers unto him.
No more shall he feel pitched and hurled
Uncomprehended into this world
For every place shall be his place,
And he shall recognize its face.
At dawn he shall upon his path;
No sword shall touch him, nor the wrath
Of the ranked crowd of clamorous men.
At even he shall home again,
And lay him down to sleep at ease,

One with the Night and the Night's peace.
Ev'n Sorrow, to be escaped of none,
But a more deep communion
Shall be to him, and Death at last
No more dreaded than the Past,
Whose shadow in the brain of earth
Informs him now and gave him birth.

Up, O Faun, up! is he a man
So dares affront the great god Pan?
Creep I now close....
(Has he not heard
Ever the lamb cry as the bird
Descends upon its helpless head
To pluck its eyes out? Blank with dread
Did he ne'er press in stumbling haste
Over the wide moor's tossing waste?
Or, stripped to plunge, did never eye
The sunned pool smiling treacherously,
Despair and terror in his heart?
Hate on him!)
See: he draws apart
That with himself he may commune
The while to a low murmuring tune
Wrung from a golden-stringëd lyre
The young men chant. Hist! Draws he nigher?

Now crouch I mid a thicket where
The spicy hedge-rose warms the air
With giddy scent, and for an hour
Woos with her open-bosomed flower
The full gaze of her lord the sun,
And through whose thorns the sunbeams run
Spangling the cavern of the brake
With chequered shade such as the snake
Loves to repose in, that the heat
Upon his sullen coils may beat,
Breeding within his ancient heart
Such malice that his tongue must dart
Flickering in silence out and in,
The while adown his withered skin,
From horns above his murderous eyes,
The cold surge shudders, ebbs, and dies.

And now yon comes, with solemn head
Sunk upon breast, with laurel spread
About his thought-bewrinkled brows.
All hail, philosopher! I rouse
Thee by a low and single hiss.
He is frozen still. A sudden bliss
Seizes me, and a branch I shake

The Faun's
Anger.

And of the Trick
the Faun played,
thereby symbolizing
the Rule of Pan
in Nature.

As gently as an unseen snake
Swinging toward him.
But he stands,
Clasps and unclasps his gradual hands
In silence save for one long sigh
Of terror.
And I draw more nigh.
Beneath his glazèd eyes I sway
Three leaves upon one stilly spray:
He blenches.
Ha! it was well done,
That final hiss.
I am alone:
For with a harsh cry he has fled
Hideously stumbling, and is led
Speechless away.
The lyre, forgot,
Lies in the grass....

XII

I know a spot   Of the Spring,
Where, to the sound of water sighing,   Frequent Haunt
The Naiads, when the sun is lying   of the Lonely
Heavy on mead and fronded tree,   Naiads.
When birds are silent and the bee
Swoons in the dewed heart of the rose,
Sing hushedly.
I will repose
Upon its banks and to the spring
An answer make with hands that cling
Over this lost lyre's murmurous chords
And with their voiced quiet mingle words
Such as my shrouded soul affords
When the warm blood within my veins
Throbs heavily, and the noon sun reigns,
Who would heaven and earth unite
In one blaze of arduous light,
Till dark woods, fields, bronzed sky, and deep,
In one maniac dull dream sleep.

XIII

The Naiads. Come, ye sorrowful, and steep
Your tired brows in a nectarous sleep: THE NAIADS'
For our kisses lightlier run   MUSIC.
Than the traceries of the sun
By the lolling water cast
Up grey precipices vast,
Lifting smooth and warm and steep
Out of the palely shimmering deep.

Come, ye sorrowful, and take
Kisses that are but half awake:
For here are eyes O softer far
Than the blossom of the star
Upon the mothy twilit waters,
And here are mouths whose gentle laughters
Are but the echoes of the deep
Laughing and murmuring in its sleep.

Come, ye sorrowful, and see
The raindrops flaming goldenly
On the stream's eddies overhead
And dragonflies with drops of red
In the crisp surface of each wing
Threading slant rains that flash and sing,
Or under the water-lily's cup,
From darkling depths, roll slowly up
The bronze flanks of an ancient bream
Into the hot sun's shattered beam,
Or over a sunk tree's bubbled bole
The perch stream in a golden shoal:
Come, ye sorrowful; our deep
Holds dreams lovelier than sleep.

But if ye sons of Sorrow come
Only wishing to be numb:
Our eyes are sad as bluebell posies,
Our breasts are soft as silken roses,
And our hands are tenderer
Than the breaths that scarce can stir
The sunlit eglantine that is
Murmurous with hidden bees.
Come, ye sorrowful, and steep
Your tired brows in a nectarous sleep.

Come, ye sorrowful, for here
No voices sound but fond and clear
Of mouths as lorn as is the rose
That under water doth disclose,
Amid her crimson petals torn,
A heart as golden as the morn;
And here are tresses languorous
As the weeds wander over us,
And brows as holy and as bland
As the honey-coloured sand
Lying sun-entranced below
The lazy water's limpid flow:
Come, ye sorrowful, and steep
Your tired brows in a nectarous sleep.

Sweet water-voices! now must I   The Faun
Unto your sorrowings reply.   prepares
But hark! or ever there can sound   to reply.
On the lull air the first profound
Few murmurs of my lyre's grave strings,
A voice uprises. Who now sings
The noon's and his own tristfulness?
A slim youth in a shepherd's dress,
Yet without sheep, who careless lies
Upon the hill. His shepherd guise
Tokens, perhaps, a poet's heart
Which joys in wandering apart
From the dinned ways where chariots roll,
From the shrill sophist with his shoal
Of gapers, from the angry mart,
From the full eyes and empty heart
Of babbling women, from the neat
Aridity of paven street,
A heart that wandering, musing, sings
The joy, depth, pain of simple things:

The Youth. The earth is still; only the white sun climbs
Through the green silence of the branching limes,   MIDDAY IN
Whose linked flowers hanging from the still tree-top   ARCADIA.
Distil their soundless syrup drop by drop,
While 'twixt the starry bracket of their lips
The black bee drowsing floats and drowsing sips.
The flimsy leaves hang on the bright blue air
Calm-suspended. Deep peace is everywhere
Filled with the murmurous rumour of high noon.
Earth seems with open eyes to sink and swoon.
In the sky peace: where nothing moves
Save the sun that smiles and loves.
A quivering peace is on the grass.
Through the noon gloam butterflies pass,
White and hot blue, only to where
They can float flat and dream on the soft air....
The trees are asleep, beautiful, slumbrous trees!
Stirred only by the passion of the breeze,
That, like a warm wave welling over rocks,
Loosens and lifts the mass of drowsing locks.
Earth, too, under the profound grass
Sleeps and sleeps, and softly heaves her slumbrous mass.
The earth sleeps. Sleeps the newly-buried clay
Or doth divinity trouble it to live alway?

No voice uplifts from under the rapt crust.
The dust cries to the unregarding dust.

Over the hill the stopped notes of twin reeds
Speak like drops from an old wound that bleeds:

A yokel's pipe an ancient pastoral sings
Above the innumerable murmur of hid wings.
I hear the cadence, sorrowful and sweet,
The oldest burthen of the earth repeat:
All love, all passion, all strife, all delight
Are but the dreams that haunt earth's visioned night.
In her eternal consciousness the stir
Of Alexander is no more to her
Than you or I: being all part of dreams,
The shadowiest shadow of a thing that seems,
The images the lone pipe-player sees,
Sitting and playing to the lone, noon breeze.
One note, one life!
They sleep: soon we as these!

XIV

Now plunge I into deepest woods,
Where everlastingly there broods
Such quiet and glamour as must be
Beneath the threshing upper sea.
Here burns no sun, but tawny light
Pervades the vistas still and bright
Of mazy boles and fallen leaves....
I press yet on. At length there cleaves
The twilit hush a pillared gleam.
The leafed floor rises. 'Tis a beam
Of sunlight fallen in a dell
Beyond the mound. There will I dwell,
Soothed by sunned quietude. For there
A carved rock spouts and moists the air
With gross-mouthed pour and rising spray....
But hark! what festive cries are they   Of the
Which greet me as I top the mound?   Satyrs' Feast.
Below, dispersed and sunk around
The green and golden of the glen,
Lie satyrs; in a leafy den,
Silenus, crowned with vines and roses,
Drowses and starts, blinks, drinks, and dozes.
Banqueting dishes strew the grass,
Goblets of gold and peacock glass,
Flagons, urns, many a brimming bowl,
And horns from which the flushed fruits roll.
High o'er the feast a fronded ash
Hangs full of sunlight, and the splash
Of the spring's leap or gurgeing flow
Into the rippled pool below,
Where lilies rock, shakes up a bright
Eddy of golden tremulous light
Over the leaves. The Oread,
In a hooded lynx pelt clad,

Smiles where she lolls ... the while twin fauns
With stamping hooves and butting horns
Join combat for a dripping cup
She bears.
But now a shout goes up
At sight of me:

Satyr. "We feast, we feast;
For, lo! the flaming sun hath ceased   The Invitation.
To climb the curve of arid sky,
And his meridian holds on high,
Narrowing with his scorching beams
The chestnut's shade, exhausting streams,
Stilling the woodland singer's note,
Piercing the eyes, shrinking the throat,
Saddening the heart of man and beast.
Yet grieve not we but sprawl and feast.
Leap down, O Faun, then, from thy rocks,
Leap down to us. Bedew thy locks
With such cool spicy nards as dwell
Within this ribbed and rosy shell;
Around thy scalded temples twine
Sprays of this fountain-wetted vine,
And from this golden jorum sip
Nectarous liquor ay, and lip
Smooth nectarines, thy sunk teeth clench
In melon dripping sherds, and quench
Thy salty thirst anew in flow
Of sparkled or dark wines that glow
With sober warmth and merriment,
Until our gladdened voices blent
Awake the vigour of our feet,
And up we start the grass to beat
With fervent foot, drink, dance again,
And, ever at the loud refrain
Clashing our cups, dance on and on,
Till the noontide lull is gone."

So join I them, and drink and sup,
And fill again the great bowl up;
And, drenched thus down, spin lusty tales
Of topping bouts 'twixt men and whales;
Of the East's Emperor who hath
A pool of wine to be his bath;
Of Hercules his thirst, and how
He did all Ethiopia plough,
And plant with vines, his thirst to sate.
We will discuss the Ideal State,
Whose sky is covered by a vine,
Whose hills are cheese, whose rivers wine,
Whose trees bear loaves brown, crisp and sweet,

Whose citizens do nought but eat,
But eat and drink, drink, eat, and snore,
And eat again, and wish no more
Than so to drink, snore, eat; who find
In this true liberty of mind
And true equality, in this
Fraternity, law, earthly bliss.
So swill again and yet again,
Till a fire flushes all the brain
And, trolling lustily and long,
Each hearty throat bursts into song.

Faun and Satyrs. Avaunt, mild-eyed Melancholy!
Welcome, Mirth and mænad Folly!   A DITHYRAMB
See about the lifted bowl,   TO DIONYSOS.
Wrinkled on its bossy scroll,
Ribald nymphs and satyrs jolly
Tussle with a prancing goat;
While Silenus, kneeling, drolly
Proffers a dry bowl unto 't
Ay, and round the mazer's brim
Boisterous Mermen shouting swim,
And each burly arm lifts up,
Wine that o'erbrims its conchëd cup;
Wherefore pour a triple potion:
If such can be dry in ocean,
'Tis as Titans we must sup!

Avaunt, brow and visage pious:
None but Bacchus boys come nigh us!
Raise the bowl and shout his name:
Io, Bacchus! for a flame
Chafes in our blood, O Bromios!
Fire no water e'er could quench,
And its heat must scorify us
If with wine we do not drench.
Wherefore overbrim the cup:
This to Jove now drink I up,
Who upon thy first of days
Snátched thee and cówed thy natal blaze,
Even as 'tis now the merry
Strength of this thy vintaged berry,
That the scorching danger stays.

To the vine now! let its golden
Leaves about our brows be folden.
To the swarthy hand that trims it!
To the grape! the sun that dims it!
To the pipe that doth embolden
Purpled stamping feet to riot
O'er the vatted winepress olden!

To the cavern's depth, chill, quiet!
Last to wine's own ruddy sprite,
Wakes in rheumy eyes a light
Ay, and ripens youth to man;
Wine which more works than wisdom can;
Wine that welcomes hardy morrows;
Wine that turns to song our sorrows;
Wine the only magian!

Deep now! every bowl enhances
The world's beauty; see there dances
In the sky the leaping sun!
'Nay, can thine eye catch but one?'
'Six now spin.' 'A seventh advances,
Flares and vomits, swerves and blazes,
Now bursts and countlessly it prances,
Pulsing to my frantic paces!'
'I flame, gyrate!' 'I shoot out heat!'
'My tricked speech trips, and trip my feet!'
'The earth runs round and heav'n is wheeling!'
'I sway; I reel.' 'Earth's wrecked and reeling!'
'Dance on.' 'Earth's gone.' 'All's white and clear!'
'Ah! Ah! Behind the blaze I hear
The Oread's laughter pealing!'

Avaunt, grief! Descend, O holy
Fierce Bacchic rapture, divine folly!

XV

Forth from the forest wend I slowly,
While in my ears yet rings the holy
Dithyramb. The noon is past,
But the sun rages. There is cast
A dumbness yet o'er earth and sky.
Down to the river then will I,
Slowly about its depths to swim,
While the stream fondles every limb
And soothes its ache. Deep I will dip,
And, blowing, raise my locks, that drip
Till the slim Hyads troop to see,
And revel, too, and play with me,
Hanging my ears with humid weed
Or mounting me as water steed.
Then, musing I will on, and so
Stray to where a silver slow
River circles through the meads,
Wherein the mooching great ox feeds,
And turns a slow eye round the sky,
Wondering if he can ever die.
And there, mayhap, 'twill come to pass

Of the Faun's
Further Wanderings.

I'll hear a sweet voice in the grass,
And yet shall mark no singer nigh,
Till, gently peering, I espy
A solemn, elfish child who sits
Unseen mid towering grass, and knits
An endless, endless daisy chain,
Crooning the while some soft refrain
Her mother sings her when she closes
Her twilit eyes.

Little Girl.   Three red, red, roses
One each for father and mother, and one,
The reddest of all, for her baby son.
None for wee Amoret? Oh, none! for she
Some day, when she grows up, a red rose will be!

Then, crossed-legged mid the meadow-sweet,   Of the Faun's
I will sink down, laugh low, and greet   Converse with
Her blue, inquiring, childish eyes   a Small
With mine, sharp, merry, brown, and wise,   She-Child.
And tell her tales of Jack who slew
Ten giants; or Mirabel who flew
On a white owl to find the Prince
And give to him the Golden Quince
Would change him from a roaring bull
To a youth blithe and beautiful;
Or tales of the Goblin and the Sloth,
Who watched the moon and swore an oath
To find out what she was: how these
Explored her mines and found her cheese.

Thus will I sit and both amuse
Until I rise and beg excuse:
Off 'to El Raschid in Assyria'
Or 'the Grand-Duchess of Illyria,'
Or 'to ask the maiden moon
Why one only of her shoon
She left us last night in the sky,
And not her silver self, and why
She always climbs the self-same track?
Lets no one ever see her back?'

XVI
But neither to the moon go I
Or to the river gliding by,
But to the woods, therein to move
Among the quiet glades I love,
Desiring nought but aye to see
The beech, ash, oak, and chestnut tree....
Till I a nymph meet who persuades

Me to the broadest of the glades,
Around whose smooth and sunken space
The far woods lie. For in this place,
Deserted but for a mid-grove
Of maiden trees, bower of the dove,
Pan plays, and should the sylvans chance,
Nymphs, fauns, and sylvans, join in dance.

XVII

On either hand the slender trees   Of the Immortal
Bow to the caressing breeze,   Dance.
And shake their shocks of silver light
Against skies marbled greenish-white,
Save where, within a rent of blue,
The tilted slip of moon glints through,
Glittering upon us as we dance
With a soft extravagance
Of limbs as blonde as autumn boughs,
And gold locks floating from moony brows.
While anguished Pan the pipes doth blow
Fond and tremulous and low,
And anon the timbrel shakes.
It is his sudden heart that breaks
For springs before the world grew old,
Rich vales, and hill-tops fiery cold!
He watches the scarce moving skies,
The trees, the glittering revelries,
The moon, the dancers lemon-clad:
The world fantastical and sad.

The high-flung timbrels pulse and knock;
We follow in a dancing flock,
Touching each other's finger-tips,
While from between our parted lips
The solemn melodies repeat
The rhythm of our shaken feet.
Then faster! and the round we trace,
Hair flowing from elated face,
Eyes lit, breast bare, with lifted knees,
And hands that toss as toss the trees....
And slow again ... with cumulate motion,
As the long draw and plunge of ocean
Bursting in a cloud of spray
Up a white, deserted bay
Of the sun-circled green Bermooths,
Whose blistering sands the cool foam soothes....
Next the bewildering pipes may sing
Some simple melody of spring,
Whose cadences remember yet
Sadly lost springs that we forget.

To which as dances April rain
On a still pool where leans no stain,
Save of the cloud's pure splendour spread
Gloriously overhead,
Our fast-flickering feet shall twinkle,
And our golden anklets tinkle,
While fair arms in aery sleeves
Shiver as the poplar's leaves.

And all the while shall Pan sit by
And play, and pause, perhaps, to sigh,
Viewing the scarce-moving skies,
The hushed and glittering revelries,
The infant moon, the slender trees
Silvering to the shivery breeze,
The fair, lorn dancers lemon-clad:
The world fantastical and sad.

XVIII
Thus may we dance the light away
Of yet one more unmemoried day.
But, the dance ended, I will go
Beyond the reach of pipes that blow
A sadness thrilling through my veins....

For now within my spirit reigns   The Faun's
Shadow: before whose brooding face,   Sadness.
Silent, there trail on gliding pace
A multitude of restless Fears,
Obscure Griefs and obscurer Tears,
Bewildered Sighs, waned Phantasies,
And all disastrous Presences,
Mutely prophetic of a Woe
I know not yet, but I shall know.

Such power Pan's grief hath to oppress,
And Memory! since now I guess
Only too well that there must come
Twilight, Calamity, and Doom.

For once I saw beneath an oak
A bard so aged it seemed he woke
That moment from a sleep of years
And in his voice were sleep and tears....
Till, wide-eyed, he, raging, spake,
Rocking as when woodlands shake
Under the first urge of the wind,
Whose roaring murk lightens behind.

Prophetic Bard. "Be warned! I feel the world grow old,

And off Olympus fades the gold
Of the simple passionate sun;
And the Gods wither one by one:
Proud-eyed Apollo's bow is broken,
And throned Zeus nods nor may be woken
But by the song of spirits seven
Quiring in the midnight heaven
Of a new world no more forlorn,
Sith unto it a Babe is born,
That in a propped, thatched stable lies,
While with darkling, reverend eyes
Dusky Emperors, coifed in gold,
Kneel mid the rushy mire, and hold
Caskets of rubies, urns of myrrh,
Whose fumes enwrap the thurifer
And coil toward the high dim rafters
Where, with lutes and warbling laughters,
Clustered cherubs of rainbow feather,
Fanning the fragrant air together,
Flit in jubilant holy glee,
And make heavenly minstrelsy
To the Child their Sun, whose glow
Bathes them His cloudlets from below....
Long shall this chimed accord be heard,
Yet all earth hushed at His first word:
Then shall be seen Apollo's car
Blaze headlong like a banished star;
And the Queen of heavenly Loves
Dragged downward by her dying doves;
Vulcan, spun on a wheel, shall track
The circle of the zodiac;
Silver Artemis be lost,
To the polar blizzards tossed;
Heaven shall curdle as with blood;
The sun be swallowed in the flood;
The universe be silent save
For the low drone of winds that lave
The shadowed great world's ashen sides
As through the rustling void she glides.
Then shall there be a whisper heard
Of the Grave's Secret and its Word,
Where in black silence none shall cry
Save those who, dead-affrighted, spy
How from the murmurous graveyards creep
The figures of eternal sleep.
Last: when 'tis light men shall behold,
Beyond the crags, a flower of gold
Blossoming in a golden haze,
And, while they guess Zeus' halls now blaze
Shall in the blossom's heart descry
The saints of a new hierarchy!"

The
Prophecy.

He ceased ... and in the morning sky
Zeus' anger threatened murmurously.
I sped away. The lightning's sword
Stabbed on the forest. But the word
Abides with me. I feel its power
Most darkly in the twilit hour,
When Night's eternal shadow, cast
Over earth hushed and pale and vast,
Darkly foretells the soundless Night
In which this orb, so green, so bright,
Now spins, and which shall compass her
When on her rondure nought shall stir
But snow-whorls which the wind shall roll
From the Equator to the Pole....

For everlastingly there is   Of the Final
Something Beyond, Behind: I wis   Nature of Pan.
All Gods are haunted, and there clings,
As hound behind fled sheep, the things
Beyond the Universe's ken:
Gods haunt the Half-Gods, Half-Gods men,
And Man the brute. Gods, born of Night,
Feel a blacker appetite
Gape to devour them; Half-Gods dread
But jealous Gods; and mere men tread
Warily lest a Half-God rise
And loose on them from empty skies
Amazement, thunder, stark affright,
Famine and sudden War's thick night,
In which loud Furies hunt the Pities
Through smoke above wrecked, flaming cities.

For Pan, the Unknown God, rules all.
He shall outlive the funeral,
Change, and decay, of many Gods,
Until he, too, lets fall his rods
Of viewless power upon that minute
When Universe cowers at Infinite!

XIX

So far my mind runs, yet I see
How little faun-philosophy
Repays my heart would learn, not teach....
Better laugh long, lie, suck a peach
Couched under tiger-lily flowers
Which daze the low hot sun with showers
Of fragrance, while the dusty bee
Drones, fumbles, falls luxuriantly
Within their throats; couched, turn a song

Of flowers all the flowers among:

There is a vale beyond blue Ida's mount,
And thither often would I, piping, stray
To listen to the music of a fount
That spelt her tears out in a Dorian lay.

"Long, long ago," she wept, "Narcissus came
Wandering down the sunny-shafted glade;
Full weary was he of the lamp's gold flame
Wavering beneath the dusky colonnade.

"For at the fall of night forth from the dim
Gardens stole Echo; kneeling by his bed,
With small sweet love-words she importuned him
Who watched the lamp flame idle overhead.

"Dry was her hot flushed cheek and dark the fire
In her great eyes; her lips roamed warm and light
Over his arm; her murmurs of desire
Mixed with the many murmurs of the night.

"In vain! He came to rest and sing with me
And loll his fingers in the liquid cool,
And drop slow tears, slow tears luxuriously
Into the shadowy motion of the pool.

"With tongue scarce audible I wooed the lad,
Whispering how beneath the drumming fall
Slumbers a rapt, deep lake, so blue, so sad,
That no fish swim it, nor about it call

"Delighting birds from green-bowered shore to shore,
Nor doth the nightingale, when June begins
And the moon mounts a pattin of bright or,
Hymn her long sorrows and her lord's black sins.

"And the boy answered, answered me, and mourned
The loveliness of Echo. 'Yet,' sighed he,
'My soul is fled, and long, thou knowest, bourned
In what far dell none knoweth, love, but thee

"'Who farest thither! Sweeter to my ears
Are thy quiet voices and the gentle breast
Of rambling water sweeter than my dear's.'
Then murmured I, 'Lean lower, love, and rest.'

"There was no sound through all the sleeping wood,
Save one sharp cry from Echo, open-lipped,
Who, as she followed, from afar did spy
How to my arms my lover downward slipped.

"Softly I rocked him down into the pool,
Shutting his ears to the loud torrents' din,
And kissed and bore him through the portals cool,
And laid him sleeping the blue halls within.

"So I returned; but never to me came
Another as beautiful, nor shall come.
Lonely I flow, and, flowing, lisp his name,
Till the sky waste and all the earth be dumb."

So sang the spring, and, answering my look,
Through the dark wood from the spring's fountain-head
Flock upon flock of eyed narcissi shook,
And the brook wept in sorrow for the dead.

Ah, Death again! nothing can fend
Us from the Sibyl of the End,
Whose delight 'tis to find new forms,
Now in dull sighs, anon in storms,
Singing, and ever of the same:
The trusting heart betrayed; the flame
Whirled in a night on cities proud;
Lightnings from skies undimmed by cloud;
The wide grave yawned before swift feet;
The small success that brings defeat;
The smiling lips and deadly eyes
Of Destiny walking in disguise.

XX
But now the sun sinks I will go   Of the
Whither two full streams meet and flow, Evening River.
Murmuring as in wedded sleep
Through evening meadows dim and deep.
There will I watch the slow trout rise
At the myriad simmering flies,
And listen to the water flowing
With such faint sounds there is no knowing
Whether its spirit laughs or weeps
Among the dreams wherein it sleeps.

Sunken amid the twilight grass,
I will watch the water pass,
Weaving ever dimmer tales
And dimmer as the evening pales....
Till from the calm the silent lark
Drops to the meadows hushed and dark,
While in the stagnant silver west,
Above the tranquil poplars' crest,
There glimmers through the murky bar

The slowly climbing Hesperal Star.

Thus brooding by the hazy stream,
I shall hear the water dream
Tinkily on, and I shall see,
As my eyes close quietly.
Into a soft and long repose,
The lone star like a silver rose
Fade with me on the drifting stream
Into the quiet night of dream.

Yet sleep I not; for lo! there wakes
From the dim water-meadow brakes
A quiring: voice as if a star,
Fallen to earth from midnight far
Beyond the haze of highest cloud,
Bewailed her errëd path aloud.
It is the nightingale who sings,
Fanning soft air with whirrëd wings,
Probing the dark with jewelled eyes.
How oft, how sad, how loud she cries!
And all the echoes answer her;
The night airs through the close wood stir
The stars that through the eddies climb
Glitter; the silver waters chime;
The lily bows her dewy head....

I, too, a sudden tear have shed.
For, ah! what voice is this can make
The vagrant heart within me ache?
That stirs an ancient tenderness,
A new need to console, love, bless
All things that 'neath this warm night sky
Rejoice and suffer, age and die?
Hunger is in my heart like bliss,
I stretch my arms out and I kiss,
Gathered in sad and sweet embrace,
The whole world's dark and simple face.

XXI

I wander forth. About my feet
The sward is fresh and doubly sweet
The loved air on my salvëd brow.
Be still. Be still. For hearken: now
A second voice behind the grove
Uprises tremulous with love.
How hushed, how moody is the strain!
Pleading O, surely, not in vain!
Sombrely rises every note,
Lingers, and in dark dells remote

Of Night's Rhapsodist. (aligned right of second stanza)

Of the Second Singer. (aligned right of XXI stanza)

Echoes until another come.

Philomel herself falls dumb.

Philomel herself falls dumb,
Mindful of her shadowy home;
Of a slowly falling surge
Sounding its unending dirge
On an alien ocean's verge;
Of a rain-smitten tower that stood
Fronting the calm, pale rolling flood;
Of a slim sister's beauty glows,
Fatefuller than a midnight rose;
Of the birth, growth, and scheming dire,
Of an accursëd King's desire;
Of night-long vigil, tongueless wrack,
And the last exultation black
O'er loathly offering, feasting sour,
A fell cry in the lonely tower,
Raging pursuit, flight's vain endeavour,
And Vengeance stilling all forever.
Save the voice that nightly cries
To the slowly wheeling skies
Of unrest resolved in calm,
Time's tears fallen like a balm,
Sorrows that dead hearts have wrung,
By the sad Enthusiast sung,
Sweeter than Euphrosyne's tongue.

O tremulous voice! who is 't that shakes
The night with fervour?
Through the brakes
Softly I thread ... emerge, and now
Across the rising meadow's brow
I glimpse, beside the farther wood,
Under the shadow of its hood,
A glimmering shape that does not move.
It is the shepherd and his love:
Close, close they stand, swooning and dim;
Her shadowed face looks up at him,
Her sighing breath his forehead warms;
He sings, she leans within his arms.

The Shepherd. Now arched dark boughs hang dim and still;
The deep dew glistens up the hill;   THE SHEPHERD'S
Silence trembles. All is still.   NIGHT SONG.

Now the sweet siren of the woods,
Philomel, passionately broods,
Or, darkling, hymns love's wildest moods.

Danaë, fainting in her tower,
Feels a sudden sun swim lower,
Gasps beneath the starry shower.

Venus in the pomegranate grove
Flutters like a fluttering dove
Under young Adonis' love.

Leda longs until alight
In the reeds those wings of white
She hears beat the upper night.

Golden now the glowing moon,
Diana over Endymion
Downward bends as in a swoon.

Wherefore, since the gods agree,
Youth is sweet and Night is free,
And Love pleasure, should not we?

Song whose desire her kisses bless!   The Faun
Song that wreaks wounds no lips redress,   is struck
O wounding song! Such loneliness   with Sorrow.
Falls, like a stun blow from behind,
That my hands grope, my eyes go blind.
I gasp....
Away, Away, O heart!
Lone, wretched Faun, depart, depart;
Hide thyself, wretched, utterly,
Climb to the clouds where none may see
And mock thy causeless misery!

What joy is mine? what is 't I have:
Immortal life? would 'twere a grave.
Thus, thus to suffer world-without-end,
No love, no hope, no goal, no friend!

And the proud, morning Centaur, how
Fares he? what lot doth Fate allow?
More wretched yet! to live and be
Perfection's lone epitome.

To feel in him a fecund power,
And lack on which to spend that dower!...
I mind me now that once I heard
Wise, gentle Pan pronounce this word:
"Whoever like a God would shine
Must share the loneliness divine."
Ah! to be Gods, then, is to be
One fierce eternal agony.
Yet, being Gods, such feel no pain;

Their strength is equal to their bane.
While I, poor half-god and half-beast,
I would be man, the last and least
Of men!
O reasoning vain:
Were I but man and one in pain,
I could not by my utmost wipe
One tear away. But now this pipe
Hangs from my neck, god Pan's elect   He takes Comfort
Gift to his children to perfect   in the Uncommon
In awe, joy, grief, and loneliness.   Gift of God.
Sound, pipe, and with thy note express
All this my heart! to thee I give
All the long days that I must live.

I wander on, I fade in mist,
O peopled World, and dost thou list?
Pipe on, difficult pipes of mine;
There is something in me divine,
And it must out. For this was I
Born, and I know I cannot die
Until, perfected pipe, thou send
My utmost: God, which is

The End.

Robert Nichols – A Concise Bibliography
Invocation (1915)
Ardours and Endurances (1917)
A Faun's Holiday & Poems & Phantasies (1917)
Sonnets to Aurelia (1920)
The Smile of the Sphinx (1920)
Fantastica: Being the smile of the sphinx and other tales of imagination (1923)
Twenty Below (1926) with Jim Tully
Wings Over Europe (1928) play
Fisbo or the Looking Glass Loaned (1934) verse satire aimed at Osbert Lancaster
A Spanish Triptych (1936) poems
Such was My Singing (1942) poems